Message from Richard Cordray

Director of the CFPB

On July 21, 2011, the Consumer Financial Protection Bureau was launched as the first federal government agency solely dedicated to consumer financial protection. The Dodd-Frank Wall Street Reform and Consumer Protection Act mandated that the Bureau develop and implement a strategy to improve the financial literacy of consumers and initiatives to educate and empower consumers to make better informed financial decisions. The Bureau is pleased to provide this report describing the Bureau's strategy and the financial literacy activities it has undertaken during its first two years of operation.

In the past few years, America has been working through the aftermath of the worst financial crisis since the Great Depression. There were many causes of the crisis. But the problems experienced by many Americans were exacerbated by the growing complexity of the financial marketplace and of the decisions consumers must make to manage their finances effectively.

The mission of the Consumer Financial Protection Bureau is to make markets for consumer financial products and services work for consumers by making rules more effective, by consistently and fairly enforcing those rules, and by empowering consumers to take more control over their economic lives. Empowering people to take more control over their economic lives is absolutely essential to our mission. But consumers should not have to go it alone, without ready access to a trusted source of impartial and expert information about matters of consumer finance. The most immediate form of consumer protection is self-protection: being able to avoid problems in the first place and to know what you can do about it when you do experience a problem. We want consumers of all ages and life situations to have the opportunities and resources to improve their financial capability so they are able to navigate the financial marketplace effectively and achieve their own financial goals. To achieve that end, we have made financial education a critical component of our work, and we are committed to helping consumers increase their capability to make sound financial choices.

The CFPB is uniquely positioned to help bridge the gap between people's current levels of financial capability and the increasingly complex financial decisions they have to make. The CFPB's financial education agenda is focused on providing consumers with tools and information to develop practical skills and support sound financial decision making. These include tailored approaches to address financial decision-making circumstances for specific populations, including: servicemembers and veterans; students and young adults; older Americans; and low-income and economically vulnerable Americans.

The Bureau's strategy to increase consumers' financial literacy and capability includes foundational research, collaborative education initiatives with stakeholders who can reach consumers where they are, and providing tools and information directly to the public to help them navigate the financial choices they face. Our research program is helping us to identify, highlight, and spread effective approaches to financial education. We are working with a broad range of partners to provide decision-making supports in moments when consumers are most receptive to receiving information and developing financial decision-making skills. We are also helping consumers directly by providing innovative tools and information online, including resources like Ask CFPB, which provides nearly 1,000 questions and answers about financial products and services at consumerfinance.gov/askcfpb/.

We all have a part to play in building a nation where every consumer is financially capable. We need to sustain a national conversation about household financial issues, not just in the financial services marketplace, but throughout our communities, including in our families, schools, workplaces, and places of worship. Parents can and should talk to their children about money and how to make sound money choices. Schools must do more to teach key financial concepts and decision-making skills. Public and private employers can invest in a financially fit workplace – with benefits to both employees and employers – as we are doing at the CFPB. Places of worship can provide a safe setting for people who are struggling in their lives to seek guidance and direction about how to make responsible financial decisions that are sustainable over time.

As the American economy continues to recover, we want consumers to be able to look ahead with renewed hope and resilience. By working in coordination with all those who are dedicated to achieving these goals, we can enhance the financial capability of everyone in America. Money decisions should support the hopes, dreams, and life goals of individuals and families. It takes both a financially capable populace and a well-policed marketplace to achieve that end. This report shows the progress the Bureau has contributed toward that national goal in our first two years. As we move forward, this important work will benefit consumers, strengthen the economy, and foster a brighter future for our country.

Sincerely,

Richard Cordray

Table of contents

Message from Richard Cordray 3

Executive summary 8

1. Introduction 13

    1.1 Financial education mandate: educate and empower consumers to make better informed financial decisions 14

    1.2 Special population offices and the Office of Consumer Engagement 15

    1.3 Financial education efforts across the Bureau 18

2. Financial literacy strategy 21

    2.1 The need for financial literacy and capability 21

    2.2 The Bureau's financial literacy strategy 22

    2.3 Consultation with FLEC and alignment with the National Strategy 25

3. Financial education initiatives: developing financial capability 27

    3.1 Bureau tools and resources 28

    3.2 Collaborative initiatives 33

4. Research and innovation: identifying what works 44

    4.1 Financial education evaluation project 46

    4.2 Measuring financial well-being 47

 4.3 Building financial capability through product design and program delivery 48

 4.4 Innovation pilots project 48

5. Outreach: sharing information and forging relationships to reach consumers 50

 5.1 Financial education 51

 5.2 Servicemembers 53

 5.3 Students 54

 5.4 Older Americans 55

 5.5 Traditionally underserved consumers 56

6. Conclusion 58

Executive summary

The recent economic downturn raised awareness about the complexity of both our financial marketplace and the decisions consumers must make to manage their finances effectively. Despite the availability of a wide range of information about managing money and about financial products and services, many consumers still struggle to make the financial decisions that serve their life goals. The Bureau hears every day from people experiencing difficulty in their financial lives, who often express regret that they did not know more about the risks involved in particular financial decisions at the time they made those decisions.

The Dodd-Frank Wall Street Reform and Consumer Protection Act mandates that the Bureau work to improve the financial literacy of American consumers. In its first two years, the Bureau has developed a strategy and a broad range of initiatives to help consumers make informed financial decisions to meet their own life goals. Broadly, this strategy recognizes that financial literacy, or financial capability, requires more than simply providing consumers with more information. Being able to manage one's financial life and make the financial decisions that will serve one's life goals requires a combination of knowledge, skills, and action. For that reason, the Bureau has pursued a strategy that focuses on identifying how, where, when, and through whom we can provide assistance to consumers for maximum benefit, and developing and implementing initiatives to carry out the approaches we identify.

> The Bureau hears every day from people experiencing difficulty in their financial lives.

There are three dimensions of the Bureau's strategy to improve financial literacy. First, we are seeking to provide assistance to consumers at specific important points in their financial lives. Second, we are engaged in research to identify effective approaches to financial education and to better define the metrics for success in financial education. Finally, we are engaged in significant ongoing outreach to a broad range of stakeholders who can assist us in reaching the public and fine-tuning our approaches.

The Bureau's financial education strategy focuses on identifying opportune moments to engage consumers about their financial decisions and providing information, tools, or other decision-making supports to help with those decisions. The Bureau is targeting its direct-to-consumer educational tools and resources towards assisting consumers with the financial aspects of large life decisions, such as going to college, retiring, or buying a home; and on smaller decisions that can have large life consequences, such as starting a habit of savings, managing debt, and passing along financial life skills to one's children.

We are aiming to provide consumers with financial decision-making resources and skills that will serve them today and in the future. We place a significant focus on answering the questions that members of the public pose to the Bureau. We are working to engage the public directly, while also collaborating with stakeholders and using existing service delivery channels. We are working to address financial decision-making issues that affect consumers generally, and also issues that affect specific populations – servicemembers, students, older Americans, and traditionally underserved consumers.

As a data-driven agency, the Bureau believes that evidence-based research is a necessary underpinning to improving the effectiveness of financial education initiatives. The Bureau has developed and implemented a financial education research program that focuses on (1) determining how to measure financial well-being and identifying the knowledge, skills, and habits associated with financially capable consumers, (2) evaluating the effectiveness of existing approaches to improving financial capability, and (3) developing and evaluating new approaches. The Bureau will use the results of this research to inform its financial education work. We will also share the results widely with other government agencies, financial education practitioners, and other stakeholders who will be able to look to the Bureau's research findings to develop policies and programs that lead to better financial outcomes for American consumers.

Finally, in order to develop and hone approaches that are effective, the Bureau is engaging in a rich and ongoing dialogue with consumers and other stakeholders to share information and learn about promising practices. Stakeholder organizations include financial education providers; federal, state, and local government agencies; financial institutions; and various other private and non-profit organizations. This outreach work both informs our strategy on an ongoing basis and enables us to forge meaningful and productive relationships with a network of organizations that will be essential conduits to reach and assist the public.

HIGHLIGHTS OF EDUCATION INITIATIVES

The CFPB, acting primarily through our Division of Consumer Education and Engagement, has undertaken a broad array of education initiatives in the last two years to implement its financial literacy strategy. Here are some highlights of these initiatives.

CFPB tools and information to assist consumers directly in making financial decisions:

- Ask CFPB (consumerfinance.gov/askcfpb/) is an interactive online tool that gives consumers answers to almost 1,000 questions about financial products and services, including credit cards, mortgages, student loans, bank accounts, credit reports, payday loans, and debt collection.

- Paying for College (consumerfinance.gov/paying-for-college/) is a suite of online tools for students and families evaluating their higher education financing options when comparing college costs, shopping for financial aid, and assessing repayment options.

- CFPB en Español (consumerfinance.gov/es/) makes CFPB resources available in Spanish.

Initiatives through community institutions:

- Schools provide the opportunity to transform the financial lives of a generation of Americans by introducing key money and finance-related concepts early, and building on that foundation consistently through the K-12 school years. The Bureau has launched a K-12 initiative to build on existing efforts to integrate financial education into K-12 curricula, and to facilitate appropriate teacher training.

- Workplaces, including the federal government, can play an important role in promoting positive saving and investing habits for their employees. The Bureau is developing an empirically-based workplace financial education program, which we will share with other federal agencies, as well as with state and local governments and private sector employers.

- Faith communities and other neighborhood organizations often serve as first responders in times of financial crisis for American families. The Bureau is working to inform these organizations about CFPB resources and plans to offer financial capability training to them, to enhance their ability to assist their members.

Collaborations with other government agencies and other organizations with existing service delivery programs or consumer relationships:

- Volunteer Income Tax Assistance (VITA) sites provide assistance to millions of low-income consumers each year in preparing their tax filings and applying for their Earned Income Tax Credit (EITC) refund. The Bureau has provided materials to VITA sites to use to encourage consumers to pre-commit to saving a portion of their EITC refund at the time they learn the amount of their refund.

- We are developing a toolkit for front-line staff in social service organizations to help them incorporate money management and financial literacy information and tools into their work with their clients. This toolkit should be useful in job training programs and other types of social services for individuals for whom financial problems may be interwoven with other types of problems for which they are seeking assistance from a social service agency.

- In coordination with the Department of Defense, we developed financial planning materials to be delivered as a component of an existing DoD program for servicemembers leaving the military, and are developing a financial education program for new recruits. These programs are designed to provide servicemembers with targeted assistance at these crucial junctures.

- To enhance protection for older consumers and others who are financially vulnerable, we are developing how-to guides for "lay fiduciaries" – people who handle financial affairs for others. We plan to make the guides available through a multitude of channels that are likely to reach people when they first take on these responsibilities. These channels include banks and credit unions that help people set up fiduciary bank accounts, elder law and trusts and estates attorneys who help people establish trusts or powers of attorney, and state courts that appoint individuals as guardians.

- Together with the Federal Deposit Insurance Corporation, we developed a financial education curriculum, Money Smart for Older Adults (MSOA), as a module in the FDIC's Money Smart financial education program. MSOA provides information for older adults and their caregivers on preventing and responding to financial exploitation. It includes tips to avoid scams, information about how to guard against identity theft and other forms of financial exploitation, and resources on how to prepare financially for unexpected life events and disasters. MSOA will be offered by community organizations around the country that interact with older adults, family members, or caregivers. Participant guides are available for download at files.consumerfinance.gov/f/201306_cfpb_msoa-participant-guide.pdf, and available for order through promotions.usa.gov/cfpbpubs.html. Community organizations that wish to offer the course in their communities can order the instructor materials from the FDIC at fdic.gov/consumers/consumer/moneysmart/olderadult.html.

1. Introduction

The Dodd-Frank Wall Street Reform and Consumer Protection Act (Dodd-Frank Act) mandates that the Director of the Consumer Financial Protection Bureau (CFPB or Bureau) submit a report, no later than 24 months after the designated transfer date, and annually thereafter, on the Bureau's activities and strategy to improve the financial literacy of consumers to the Committee on Banking, Housing, and Urban Affairs of the Senate, and the Committee on Financial Services of the House of Representatives.[1] The Bureau is pleased to submit this inaugural report on the Bureau's financial literacy work. The report covers the time period from July 21, 2011, when the Bureau opened its doors, through June 15, 2013.

The economic crisis that led to passage of the Dodd-Frank Act demonstrated that national financial stability can depend on the financial well-being of individuals and families. The Bureau is the nation's first federal agency focused solely on consumer financial protection. Created by the Dodd-Frank Act, the Bureau's mission is to help consumer financial markets work for American consumers, responsible providers, and the economy as a whole,

> **Enhancing financial literacy is an integral part of the Bureau's consumer financial protection function.**

- by making rules more effective;
- by consistently and fairly enforcing those rules; and
- by empowering consumers to take more control over their economic lives.

---

[1] Consumer Financial Protection Act of 2010, Pub. L. No. 111-203, § 1013(d)(4), 124 Stat. 1955, 1971 (codified at 12 U.S.C. § 5493(d)(4)).

Enhancing financial literacy is an integral part of the Bureau's consumer financial protection function. This mandate is reflected in numerous provisions of the Dodd-Frank Act that charge the Bureau with researching, developing, promoting, and implementing financial literacy programs and activities. These include provisions directing the establishment of the Office of Financial Education (OFE), which is responsible for developing and implementing a strategy and a broad range of initiatives to provide individuals and families with opportunities to access information, education, tools, and services to make better informed financial decisions. The Dodd-Frank Act also mandated the creation of offices or functions addressing special consumer populations, as described further below.

The Bureau's financial literacy work is performed chiefly through our Division of Consumer Education and Engagement (CEE). This division includes the Office of Financial Education, the Office of Consumer Engagement, which develops the Bureau's online relationship with consumers, and the four offices that address issues and needs, including financial education, of special populations: the Office for Servicemember Affairs, the Office for Students, the Office of Financial Protection for Older Americans, and the Office of Financial Empowerment, serving traditionally underserved consumers.

Each of these six offices plays a role in implementing the Bureau's strategy to provide financial education and enhance financial literacy and capability. Other parts of the Bureau also contribute to our financial education mission. For example, the Bureau's Office of Research is a CEE partner in the research elements of the Bureau's financial education strategy. The Bureau's Office of Fair Lending and Equal Opportunity and Office of Consumer Response also provide education to the public. The Bureau's Know Before You Owe initiatives, as well as many other financial education initiatives, rely on cross-Bureau subject-matter expertise. The Office of Community Affairs from the Division of External Affairs works with CEE offices to engage consumers and organizations through webinars and other public events.

1.1 Financial education mandate: educate and empower consumers to make better informed financial decisions

The Bureau's principal financial literacy mandate is set forth in § 1013(d)(1) of the Dodd-Frank Act. Section 1013(d)(1) mandated establishment of an Office of Financial Education to "be responsible for developing and implementing initiatives intended to educate and empower consumers to make better informed financial decisions."[2] Further, the statute directs OFE to "develop and implement a strategy to improve the financial literacy of consumers that includes measurable goals and objectives, in consultation with the Financial Literacy and Education Commission, consistent with the National Strategy for Financial Literacy, through activities including providing opportunities for consumers to access" various types of information, education, tools, and services.[3] OFE is also responsible, with the Bureau's Office of Research, for conducting research related to financial education and counseling.[4]

1.2 Special population offices and the Office of Consumer Engagement

The Dodd-Frank Act also mandated creation of offices to develop financial education and policy initiatives to support the financial well-being of particular segments of the consumer population. These offices focus on servicemembers, students, older Americans, and "traditionally underserved" consumers.

SERVICEMEMBERS

The Dodd-Frank Act mandated the establishment of an Office of Servicemember Affairs to "be responsible for developing and implementing initiatives for service members and their families," including initiatives intended to "educate and empower service members and their families to make better informed decisions regarding consumer financial products and services."[5] The Office of Servicemember Affairs works to improve consumer financial protection for servicemembers, veterans, and their families in a number of ways. The Office partners with the Department of Defense and the Department of Veterans Affairs to provide opportunities for

---

[2] 12 U.S.C. § 5493(d)(1).

[3] 12 U.S.C. § 5493(d)(2).

[4] 12 U.S.C. § 5493(d)(3)(B).

[5] 12 U.S.C. § 5493(e)(1)(A).

servicemembers, veterans, and their families to receive financial education relevant to their needs. The Office monitors complaints submitted by servicemembers, veterans, and their families. The Office coordinates consumer protection efforts among federal and state agencies related to consumer financial products and services offered to, or used by, military families.[6]

STUDENTS

The Dodd-Frank Act directed the Secretary of the Treasury, in consultation with the Bureau's Director, to designate a Private Education Loan Ombudsman within the Bureau "to provide timely assistance to borrowers of private education loans."[7] The Private Education Loan Ombudsman position is held by the Assistant Director of the Office for Students. The Office for Students works to enhance the ability of students and younger consumers to make financial decisions, including monitoring complaints about private student loans, providing information and tools to help students understand the risks from student loans and other financial products, and identifying policy and marketplace issues with special impact on students and younger consumers.[8]

OLDER AMERICANS

The Dodd-Frank Act mandated establishment of an Office of Financial Protection for Older Americans (Office for Older Americans). The functions of the Office for Older Americans include "activities designed to facilitate the financial literacy of individuals who have attained the age of 62 years or more . . . on protection from unfair, deceptive, and abusive practices and on current and future financial choices, including through the dissemination of materials to seniors on such topics."[9] More specifically, the statute directs the Office for Older Americans to, among other things, (1) develop goals for financial literacy and counseling programs for seniors, including programs that "help seniors recognize warning signs of unfair, deceptive, or abusive practices" and "protect themselves from such practices," and programs that "provide one-on-one financial

---

[6] 12 U.S.C. § 5493(e)(1).

[7] 12 U.S.C. § 5535(a).

[8] 12 U.S.C. § 5535(c).

[9] 12 U.S.C. § 5493(g)(1).

counseling on issues including long-term savings and later-life economic security"; and (2) "conduct research to identify best practices and effective methods, tools, technology and strategies to educate and counsel seniors about personal finance management...."[10] The statute also directs the Office for Older Americans to work with community organizations and other entities that educate and assist older consumers.

TRADITIONALLY UNDERSERVED CONSUMERS

The Dodd-Frank Act mandated establishment of a unit whose functions are to include providing "information, guidance, and technical assistance regarding the offering and provision of consumer financial products or services to traditionally underserved consumers and communities."[11] The term "traditionally underserved consumers" includes un-banked and under-banked consumers.[12] The Office of Financial Empowerment (Empowerment) directs its efforts towards strengthening financial consumer protection and enhancing the financial capability of low-income and other economically vulnerable consumers who comprise the traditionally underserved.

OFFICE OF CONSUMER ENGAGEMENT

The Office of Consumer Engagement (Consumer Engagement) develops resources, information, and online tools to help consumers make better-informed financial decisions. Consumer Engagement works to create an interactive, informative relationship between the CFPB and consumers, and collaborates with offices and divisions across the Bureau on ways to effectively engage the public. Consumer Engagement approaches this mission with user-centered and data-driven approaches to public engagement.

---

[10] 12 U.S.C. § 5493(g)(3)(A)(i)-(ii); 12 U.S.C. § 5493(g)(3)(D).

[11] 12 U.S.C. § 5493(b)(2).

[12] *See* 12 U.S.C. § 5493(b)(1)(F).

1.3 Financial education efforts across the Bureau

This report principally covers the financial education work performed by the Bureau through the Division of Consumer Education and Engagement. Financial education is also an important component of the consumer protection work of Bureau offices within other divisions, such as the work described below.[13]

OFFICE OF CONSUMER RESPONSE

The Office of Consumer Response (Consumer Response), which is part of the Bureau's Operations Division, hears directly from consumers about the challenges they face in the marketplace, brings their concerns to the attention of companies, and assists in addressing their complaints.[14] Consumer Response is supported by experts from throughout the Bureau who provide subject matter expertise. In addition, the Offices of Servicemember Affairs and Students help to monitor and address complaints.

Information about consumer complaints is available to the public through the Consumer Complaint Database. The database is publicly available at consumerfinance.gov/complaintdatabase/ and serves as an additional informational tool to inform consumer decision making around financial products and services. Consumers can submit complaints at consumerfinance.gov/complaint/, or by calling 855- 411-CFPB (2372).[15]

---

[13] This work is also discussed in other reports to Congress. *See, e.g.*, Consumer Response Annual Report (Mar. 31, 2012), *available at* http://files.consumerfinance.gov/f/201204_cfpb_ConsumerResponseAnnualReport.pdf; Fair Lending Report of the Consumer Financial Protection Bureau (Dec. 2012), *available at* http://files.consumerfinance.gov/f/201212_cfpb_fair-lending-report.pdf; Annual Report of the Consumer Financial Protection Bureau Pursuant to Section 1017(e)(4) of the Dodd-Frank Act (July 2012) *available at* http://files.consumerfinance.gov/f/201207_cfpb_report_annual-to-house-appropriations-committee.pdf.

[14] 12 U.S.C. § 5493(b)(3); *see also* 12 U.S.C. § 5511(c)(2).

[15] Complaints can also be submitted by mail to Consumer Financial Protection Bureau, P.O. Box 4503, Iowa City, Iowa 52244, or by fax to 855-237-2392.

OFFICE OF FAIR LENDING AND EQUAL OPPORTUNITY

The Dodd-Frank Act charges the Office of Fair Lending and Equal Opportunity (Fair Lending), which is part of the Division of Supervision, Enforcement, and Fair Lending, with "providing oversight and enforcement of Federal laws intended to ensure the fair, equitable, and nondiscriminatory access to credit for both individuals and communities that are enforced by the Bureau . . . ."[16] Among other things, the statute directs Fair Lending to work with "private industry, fair lending, civil rights, consumer and community advocates on the promotion of fair lending compliance and education . . . ."[17] The Office of Financial Education has collaborated with Fair Lending to promote awareness of federal fair lending laws and help consumers recognize prohibited practices. In a brochure released in May 2012 called "Credit Discrimination is Illegal," the Bureau advises consumers about the Equal Credit Opportunity Act's protections, warning signs of discrimination, and how to protect themselves.[18]

KNOW BEFORE YOU OWE INITIATIVES

The Bureau seeks to make the costs, risks, and benefits of financial products and services easier for consumers to understand through a series of initiatives collectively known as Know Before You Owe. The goal of these projects is to help consumers make better informed choices about these products and services for themselves and their families. To date, the Bureau has developed prototype disclosure forms for mortgages, credit cards, and student loans, and in each case invited the public to tell us what kinds of disclosures may work best, and why. These projects use interdisciplinary expertise that spans the Bureau – including Regulations attorneys, product experts, Community Affairs staff, and technology and engagement specialists.

The Bureau's Know Before You Owe mortgages project has centered on combining the two key federal mortgage disclosures – the Truth in Lending Disclosure and the HUD-1 Settlement

---

[16] 12 U.S.C. § 5493(c)(2)(A).

[17] 12 U.S.C. § 5493(c)(2)(C).

[18] CFPB, *Know Your Rights: Credit Discrimination is Illegal*, available at
http://files.consumerfinance.gov/f/201212_cfpb_credit-discrimination-brochure.pdf.

Statement – into a single, easier-to-use form.[19] In the course of the project, the Bureau has received more than 27,000 individual comments from online participants. In the Know Before You Owe credit cards project, the Bureau has developed a prototype credit card agreement aimed at making the prices and terms easier for consumers to understand. The Bureau's Office for Students, working with other Bureau experts and the U.S. Department of Education, created the Know Before You Owe student loans project, which is discussed later in this report.

---

[19] *See* 12 U.S.C. § 5532(f).

2. Financial literacy strategy

The recent economic downturn raised awareness about the importance of individual financial capability. Financial products are numerous and complex, requiring individuals to make choices from an array of options. In addition, there are substantial costs to attaining many significant life goals, such as owning a home or sending one's child to college. Further, consumers are increasingly responsible for saving for and managing the funds for their retirement. In this context, not having the skills to make sound financial decisions can have severe consequences for Americans' abilities to reach their life goals.[20]

2.1 The need for financial literacy and capability

Recent studies provide evidence of specific ways that U.S. consumers could use help in developing effective habits and skills around money management and personal finances. According to recently released results of the 2012 National Financial Capability Study, a majority of American adults say they have not formed a savings cushion to protect them from unanticipated financial emergencies or to provide for predictable life events such as their children's college education or their own retirement. Many Americans also do not comparison shop before obtaining financial products such as a credit card. Similarly, many American adults who believe they are adept at dealing with day-to-day financial matters use credit cards in costly ways, such as paying only the minimum payment each billing cycle, making late payments,

---

[20] FINRA Investor Education Foundation, *Financial Capability in the United States: National Survey – Executive Summary* (Dec. 2009), at 4, *available at*
http://www.usfinancialcapability.org/downloads/NFCS_2009_Natl_Exec_Sum.pdf.

thereby triggering late fees, or using the cards for cash advances and other costly non-bank borrowing methods.

Financial education literature, as well as input the Bureau has received from financial education providers and academics, suggests that providing consumers with information is only part of the solution. Being able to manage one's financial life and make the financial decisions that will serve one's life goals requires a combination of knowledge, skills, and action. Together, these abilities are known as "financial literacy" or "financial capability." They include the ability to analyze the costs, risks and consequences of particular financial services, products, and decisions, make effective choices and recover from poor ones, know where to go for help, and take other actions to improve present and long-term financial well-being in an evolving financial landscape. Financial education experts also consistently suggest that more research is needed to further determine what financial education approaches are most effective in developing financial capability, and to further identify meaningful ways to measure financial knowledge, behavior, and well-being.

2.2 The Bureau's financial literacy strategy

The Bureau has developed a strategy to improve consumers' financial capability and help consumers make informed financial decisions. Broadly, the Bureau's strategy is to motivate and support consumers in taking positive action on financial decisions that serve their own life goals.[21] To this end, the Bureau is focusing on reaching consumers in those moments when the consumer is most receptive to learning about a financial decision. The Bureau's approach is to provide relevant information, tools, or other decision-making supports in those moments. The Bureau is focusing on big life decisions, such as going to college, retiring, or buying a home, and

> The Bureau's strategy is to provide consumers with relevant information, tools, or other decision-making supports in those moments when they are most receptive to learning about a financial decision.

---

[21] This financial literacy strategy is reflected in Goal 2 of the Bureau's strategic plan, which is to empower consumers to live better financial lives. *See CFPB Strategic Plan FY 2013 – FY 2017*, at 16-23, *available at* http://www.consumerfinance.gov/strategic-plan/#goal2.

smaller decisions that can have significant life consequences, such as starting to build an emergency savings cushion, managing debt, and passing on knowledge and skills in the family by talking to children about money. The Bureau's strategy includes reaching consumers directly, and working with community groups and organizations with existing networks and consumer relationships to reach people in those moments. The strategy also includes research to identify ways to enhance the effectiveness of work to improve consumers' financial capability.

The strategy has three key aspects: education initiatives, research and innovation, and outreach to key stakeholders who can help to reach the public.

EDUCATION INITIATIVES TO REACH CONSUMERS IN OPPORTUNE MOMENTS

The Bureau seeks opportunities to engage consumers at those moments when they are most receptive to learning about financial decisions. To this end, the Bureau has developed education initiatives to engage with consumers in a broad array of times and places – through CFPB tools and resources that we make available to consumers directly on the Bureau's website and elsewhere, through community intermediaries, and through collaborations with other government agencies and other organizations that offer other means to reach consumers at opportune moments. We also seek to support financial decisions today in a manner that will develop and sustain skills for decisions tomorrow. For example, students applying to college can use the Financial Aid Shopping Sheet, discussed below, to help them compare costs of various colleges as they decide where to pursue a college education. At the same time, using the Shopping Sheet for the college decision may develop comparison-shopping skills they can apply to other major purchases.

The Bureau's financial education initiatives to date are discussed in Section 3 of this report.

EVIDENCE-BASED RESEARCH AND INNOVATION TO IDENTIFY WHAT WORKS

In order to improve consumers' capability to make financial decisions to reach their own life goals, the Bureau seeks to further expand the base of knowledge about what works to achieve positive financial outcomes, for use by the Bureau and by other providers of financial education. To this end, the Bureau is conducting evidence-based research to build on current knowledge of what approaches to financial education are effective and how to measure effectiveness. The current projects focus on (1) determining how to measure financial well-being and identifying the knowledge, skills, and habits associated with financially capable consumers, (2) evaluating the effectiveness of existing approaches to improving financial decision making and outcomes, and (3) developing and evaluating new approaches. The Bureau will use the results of this research to inform its financial education work, and will also share the results widely with other government agencies, financial education practitioners, and other stakeholders. In this way, the Bureau's research findings can also support development of effective policies and programs by others involved in financial education.

Our financial education research and innovation work is discussed in Section 4 of this report.

OUTREACH TO SHARE INFORMATION AND DEVELOP APPROACHES AND COLLABORATIONS TO REACH CONSUMERS

The Bureau is engaging in broad and varied outreach with consumers and other stakeholders to build relationships, share information and promising practices, and ultimately to reach a larger portion of the American public with effective financial education resources. The Bureau engages in dialogue with consumers to understand their needs and to make the Bureau known as a trusted resource for reliable information and tools. The Bureau also uses outreach to build a stakeholder network for sharing best practices and information, and to develop relationships with organizations that can reach consumers. These organizations include financial education providers, federal, state, and local government agencies, financial service providers, and various other types of private and non-profit organizations. Through this ongoing dialogue, we inform our financial education strategy and initiatives, and connect to the network through which we can reach consumers with targeted and meaningful assistance and information.

The Bureau's financial education outreach activities are discussed in Section 5 of this report.

2.2.1 Measurable performance goals

The Bureau incorporates measurable performance goals and objectives into its financial education, research, and outreach initiatives, as it does with all of its work, in order to measure the effectiveness of its efforts. For example, the Bureau tracks metrics on usage of online resources, such as the number of unique visits and views to areas of the Bureau's website that provide consumer tools, information, and assistance. When we offer new resources or materials through third-party existing programs, we measure the numbers of persons served through the programs. The Bureau is evaluating additional ways to assess the impact of its financial education efforts. The Bureau's financial well-being metrics project, discussed below, will identify what knowledge and other factors affect financial well-being and how to measure these factors. We will use the knowledge yielded by this research to promote enhanced financial education and financial capability work, and further hone and target our own financial education efforts.

2.3 Consultation with FLEC and alignment with the National Strategy

The Bureau's strategy to improve the financial literacy of consumers has been informed by its consultations with the Financial Literacy and Education Commission (FLEC or Commission). Congress established the Commission in 2003 with the mandate to improve the financial literacy and education of Americans, and to coordinate financial education efforts in the federal government through, among other things, development of a national strategy to promote financial literacy and education.[22] The Commission currently comprises 21 federal agencies and the White House Domestic Policy Council. It is chaired by the Secretary of the Treasury, and the Bureau's Director serves as Vice-Chair.[23]

In addition to its role as Vice-Chair, the Bureau is an active member of the Commission's Leadership Committee and work groups. In these capacities and in its own work, the Bureau is actively engaged in furthering the National Strategy for Financial Literacy (National Strategy) and FLEC's current "Starting Early for Financial Success" strategic focus. The Starting Early strategic focus is intended to serve as a vehicle for achieving coordination of resources and activities among Commission member agencies, as well as with other levels of government and the private and non-profit sectors.[24] A number of the Bureau's activities are aligned with this initiative, including its K-12 initiative, Foundations workplace initiative, and Paying for College tools. In addition, the Bureau's financial education research initiatives are consistent with the Commission's research priorities.[25]

---

[22] *See* Financial Literacy and Education Improvement Act, Pub. L. No. 108-159, Tit. V, § 511, 117 Stat. 2003 (codified at 20 U.S.C. §§ 9701-9709).

[23] Consumer Financial Protection Act of 2010, Pub. L. No. 111-203, § 1013(d)(5), (6), 124 Stat. 1955, 1971 (codified at 20 U.S.C. § 9702(c)(1)(C), (d)); *see* http://www.treasury.gov/resource-center/financial-education/Pages/commission-index.aspx (last visited June 27, 2013).

[24] *See* Financial Literacy & Education Commission, Minutes of Public Meeting (Oct. 18, 2012), *available at* http://www.treasury.gov/resource-center/financial-education/Documents/Minutes%2010%2018%2012.pdf.

[25] Financial Literacy & Education Commission, Research Priorities Applied to the 2013-2014 Strategic Focus, "Starting Early for Financial Success" (May 2013), *available at* http://www.treasury.gov/resource-

The Bureau's strategy also aligns with each of the National Strategy goals for moving the nation towards the vision of sustained financial well-being for all individuals and families in the United States.[26] The first goal of the National Strategy is to "increase awareness of and access to financial education." The Bureau's strategy likewise seeks to provide individuals and families with access to reliable, clear, timely, relevant, and effective financial information and educational resources disseminated through many different channels, such as schools, employers, and financial education providers.

The second goal of the National Strategy is to "determine and integrate core financial competencies." Core competencies are basic topic areas in financial management: earning, spending, saving and investing, borrowing, and protecting against risk. The Bureau's strategy includes providing tools and informational resources that develop and enhance consumers' competency in these basic areas of managing their personal finances.

The third goal of the National Strategy is to "improve financial education infrastructure." The Bureau's strategy relies on developing a broad variety of collaborations with other governmental, private, and non-profit organizations to reach consumers. These collaborations will create or build on existing infrastructure for delivering financial education to diverse constituencies and sharing information.

Goal four of the National Strategy is to "identify, enhance, and share effective practices." The Bureau's strategy is to use evidence-based approaches in its financial education initiatives. In order to do this, the Bureau is conducting rigorous research and evaluation of financial literacy and education strategies and metrics, and will share its learning widely. These elements of the National Strategy are reflected more specifically in the Bureau's education, research, and outreach initiatives described below.

---

center/financial-education/Documents/Starting%20Early%20Research%20Priorities%20May%202013.pdf; Financial Literacy & Education Commission, Research and Evaluation Working Group, 2012 Research Priorities and Research Questions, *available at* http://www.treasury.gov/resource-center/financial-education/Documents/2012%20Research%20Priorities%20-%20May%2012.pdf. Financial Education staff serve on the Commission's Research and Evaluation Working Group, which has developed these research priorities to coordinate research efforts among the FLEC agencies. The Bureau's financial education research work is discussed below.

[26] *See* Financial Literacy & Education Commission, Promoting Financial Success in the United States: National Strategy for Financial Literacy 2011, at 8-12, *available at* http://www.treasury.gov/resource-center/financial-education/Documents/NationalStrategyBook_12310%20(2).pdf.

3. Financial education initiatives: developing financial capability

The Bureau has developed a broad range of education initiatives to implement its financial literacy strategy. These initiatives are designed to provide consumers with actionable financial information and tools at specific important moments in their financial lives, and with opportunities to develop the skills to navigate the financial marketplace and manage their financial lives effectively. The Bureau is approaching this task in two ways. First, the Bureau is engaging consumers directly through interactive tools, social media, a CFPB digital library of consumer information, and CFPB print publications. Second, the Bureau is reaching consumers through collaborative initiatives that leverage existing public, private, and non-profit resources and efforts.

The Bureau's financial education initiatives are designed to provide consumers with opportunities to access a broad range of financial information, tools, services, and other resources to support financial capability. These include providing opportunities to access information or activities to assist with evaluating credit products such as mortgages, credit cards, or student loans; preparing for education expenses and other major purchases; reducing debt and improving the consumer's financial situation; developing long-

> **The Bureau has developed education initiatives to engage with consumers at specific important points in their financial lives.**

term savings strategies; saving at the time of income tax filing; and providing opportunities to access savings, borrowing, and other services found at mainstream financial institutions.[27]

3.1 Bureau tools and resources

The Bureau has developed extensive resources to provide consumers directly with impartial information about the financial marketplace and tools for financial decision making. Highlights of these initiatives are described below.

3.1.1 Ask CFPB

In March 2012, the Bureau launched Ask CFPB, an interactive online tool that gives consumers answers to almost 1,000 questions about financial products and services, including credit cards, mortgages, student loans, bank accounts, credit reports, payday loans, and debt collection. Ask CFPB is available at consumerfinance.gov/askcfpb/. The Bureau has gradually added product categories to Ask CFPB as it has developed questions and answers to respond to consumer questions or to support the handling of complaints in those areas. Consumers can navigate Ask CFPB by typing in their own search words or choosing a financial product category. Consumers can narrow a search to specific topics, such as "credit report" or "debit card" from any search page. Consumers can also access information about financial issues applicable to specific populations, such as servicemembers, students, older Americans, or parents.

> Ask CFPB is an interactive online tool that gives consumers answers to almost 1,000 questions about financial products and services.

The vast majority of consumers access Ask CFPB from Internet search engines. The major search engines rank Ask CFPB high among the array of consumer financial advice available online, which is an indicator of its utility to consumers. For example, Google lists Ask CFPB as the first answer when a consumer searches for "Where can I get my credit score?" Consumers

---

[27] See 12 U.S.C. § 5493(d)(2).

can also get answers to their questions about these financial products and services by calling the CFPB toll-free at 855- 411-CFPB (2372).

3.1.2 Consumer Experience Program

PAYING FOR COLLEGE

Paying for College is a suite of online tools targeted to students and families evaluating their options when financing a higher education. The tools address the entire lifecycle of financing college, from comparing college costs, to shopping for financial aid, through assessing options to repay student loan debt after graduation.

Choose a Loan

Choose a Loan is an interactive guide designed to help students and families understand their options for financing the costs of college. This tool allows consumers to see the future costs and risks of different financing options, in order to enable them to make informed choices. For example, private student loans may not offer the same consumer protections as federal loans and are generally more expensive for borrowers. The guide includes expert advice on the different types of student loans, and a plain-language explanation of the terms, conditions, costs, and fees associated with these different products. This feature also includes a printable one-page "action guide" that users can bring with them when evaluating financing options.

> Paying for College is a suite of online tools targeted to students and families evaluating their options when financing a higher education.

Compare Financial Aid

The financial aid offer letters that prospective students receive from schools can be confusing, and the descriptions of the different types of financial aid that are available can vary widely. Compare Financial Aid allows users to make apples-to-apples comparisons among financial aid offers from different colleges and universities. Users can take the financial aid offer letters provided by their schools and build a personalized visualization of the costs of financing college—including an estimate of the monthly payment upon graduation that would be required to pay back the combined types of financial aid. This tool relies on data from the U.S. Department of Education to fill in information that may not be included in the applicant's financial aid offer letter, giving users a more complete picture of their options. It also includes a feature designed to assist servicemembers, veterans, and their families in accessing information about military educational benefits to which they may be entitled.

In April 2012, the Bureau released a prototype of Compare Financial Aid and asked the public to provide feedback. We received input from students and parents across the country, as well as high school guidance counselors, financial aid administrators, and other experts. We integrated their feedback into subsequent iterations of Compare Financial Aid, releasing the latest version in April 2013.

Repay Student Debt

Millions of borrowers are currently repaying federal and private student loans. Many borrowers are eligible for a wide range of alternative repayment plans and other consumer protections, but they may not understand their options. Repay Student Debt guides users through a series of questions and provides a set of recommendations tailored to their answers. Borrowers can learn more about repayment options that may lower their monthly payment or provide short-term relief if they run into trouble; and borrowers in default can learn about options that might hold the key to repairing their credit, going back to school, or bringing their loans back into good standing. The Bureau launched a prototype of this tool in October 2011. Based on user feedback, in July 2012, we launched a separate tool for borrowers in default and facing debt collection. In December 2012, the Bureau launched the full-featured version of Repay Student Debt designed to assist all borrowers in repayment.

Manage Your College Money

Manage Your College Money is an interactive guide for college students and prospective college students to help inform what may be their first major choices in the financial services marketplace. Users can learn about financial aid disbursement options and bank accounts, and the costs and risks associated with these products. College students and prospective college students can use Manage Your College Money to help them get settled financially even before they get to campus.

3.1.3 CFPB en Español

According to Census data, 37 million people in the U.S. primarily speak Spanish at home.[28] Recognizing that at least some portion of this population could be well served by Spanish language resources, the Bureau launched CFPB en Español, a Bureau website that provides Spanish-speaking consumers a central point of access to the Bureau's resources available in Spanish. The website has four major components: a homepage that highlights CFPB services; Ask CFPB content in Spanish; a complaints page that highlights the phone number consumers can call to submit a complaint in Spanish; and an About Us page that features a Spanish-language video and introductory content about how the CFPB works to protect consumers. The website was created using responsive design, meaning it is optimized for use on both mobile devices and computers in order to better serve all consumers. The website launched in May 2013 and is available at consumerfinance.gov/es/.

> CFPB en Español provides a central point of access to CFPB online resources available in Spanish.

3.1.4 K-12 parent education tools

The Offices of Financial Education and Consumer Engagement launched a parent education campaign in April 2013 to engage parents and guardians in the financial education of their children by encouraging discussion of money management topics at home and providing tools for parents to have money conversations with their children. We offer a set of Ask CFPB questions and answers especially for parents, which is available by going to consumerfinance.gov/askcfpb/ and clicking on the

> We offer a set of Ask CFPB questions and answers to help parents teach their children about money basics.

---

[28] U.S. Census Bureau, Language Spoken at Home by Ability to Speak English for the Population 5 Years and Over, http://factfinder2.census.gov/faces/tableservices/jsf/pages/productview.xhtml?pid=ACS_10_1YR_B16001&prodType=table (last visited June 27, 2013).

"Especially for" link for Parents, or at
http://www.consumerfinance.gov/askcfpb/search?q=&selected_facets=audience_exact%3AParents. We hosted a Twitter chat with Bureau staff and financial experts focused on how to have the "money talk" with kids. We also released a Pinterest graphic for parents to use in teaching kids to save and plan for items they want to purchase. This campaign is part of the Office of Financial Education's K-12 initiative, discussed below.

3.1.5 Publications

GENERAL

The Office of Financial Education has created a range of publications for consumers that provide straightforward information about money management and other financial issues. These publications include brochures about how to avoid foreclosure, what to do if you cannot pay your credit card bills, checking your credit report, avoiding checking account fees, tax-time saving, and other topics. In collaboration with the Office of Fair Lending and Equal Opportunity, the Office of Financial Education created a brochure on how to protect against credit discrimination. The Bureau makes most of these resources available in both English and Spanish, provides them for download or bulk ordering at promotions.usa.gov/cfpbpubs.html, and distributes them at Bureau public events. As of May 31, 2013, the Bureau had distributed over 198,000 copies of its publications and over 25,000 had been downloaded. The three most popular resources ordered to date have been Check Your Credit Report, Save Some and Spend Some, and Pay Attention to Your Credit Report.

OLDER AMERICANS

Reverse mortgage guide
The Office for Older Americans developed a plain language guide to reverse mortgages for consumers, with input from subject matter experts in the Bureau's Research, Markets and Regulations Division. The guide highlights key decision points to help potential reverse mortgage borrowers assess the financial ramifications of securing a reverse mortgage, including payout and product options and alternatives. The guide is available on the CFPB website at http://files.consumerfinance.gov/f/201206_cfpb_Reverse_Mortgage_Guidance.pdf and through other federal agencies, non-profit organizations, and housing counselors throughout the country.

Senior designations report and guide

In April 2013, the Office for Older Americans released a report to Congress and the U.S. Securities and Exchange Commission entitled Senior Designations for Financial Advisers: Reducing Consumer Confusion and Risks, which is available at files.consumerfinance.gov/f/201304_CFPB_OlderAmericans_Report.pdf.[29] The report describes consumer confusion surrounding the wide variety of designations used by financial advisers to signify expertise in senior financial issues. The report includes recommendations to help older consumers verify credentials, improve the consistency of standards for acquiring the credentials, improve the consistency of standards for conduct of designees, and reduce consumer confusion. The Office for Older Americans expects to release a consumer guide to help older consumers understand and verify senior designation and certification titles later in 2013.

Lay fiduciaries guide

The Office for Older Americans is producing user-friendly how-to guides for agents acting under powers of attorney, guardians, trustees, Social Security representative payees, Veterans Affairs fiduciaries, and others who may handle financial affairs for older Americans and other vulnerable adults. Family members and others serving as fiduciaries often have no experience handling someone else's money. The materials include a set of generic national guides, state-specific guides for six states, and a replication manual for other states. The guides explain what a fiduciary does, record-keeping and prudent investment requirements, limitations on commingling funds, and other critical basics for managing a vulnerable adult's money. The guides also cover how to spot financial exploitation and protect assets from unfair, deceptive, and abusive practices by third parties. The guides are expected to be released in 2013.

3.2 Collaborative initiatives

In order to reach consumers, the Bureau is developing collaborations with a broad range of partners and intermediaries, including other federal agencies; state, local, and tribal governments; private and non-profit organizations; and schools, workplaces, and faith

---

[29] CFPB, *Senior Designations for Financial Advisers: Reducing Consumer Confusion and Risks* (April 18, 2013), *available at* files.consumerfinance.gov/f/201304_CFPB_OlderAmericans_Report.pdf.

communities and other neighborhood organizations. These collaborative initiatives take many forms. In general, the Bureau seeks to design financial education initiatives in a manner that leverages and complements effective federal and other efforts already underway, or utilizes the partner or intermediary's unique resources, expertise, consumer relationships, or infrastructure to reach consumers at opportune times with relevant information, tools, or other supports.[30]

3.2.1 Tax-time savings: collaboration with Volunteer Income Tax Assistance sites

The Offices of Financial Education and Financial Empowerment developed an initiative to encourage Earned Income Tax Credit (EITC)-eligible recipients to save some portion of their EITC refunds as a seed to grow savings. The EITC is a refundable tax credit, and for many low-to-moderate income families represents the largest lump sum of money they will receive all year. The initiative uses the free tax preparation services offered through Volunteer Income Tax Assistance (VITA) sites to reach EITC-eligible individuals and families at an ideal moment in their financial lives – when they learn the amount of their EITC credit and expected tax refund.[31] The initiative also encourages the use of free tax preparation services, and the use of electronic filing and direct deposit as an alternative to more expensive products and services. This initiative fulfills a statutory mandate for the Office of Financial Education, to provide consumers with wealth building strategies and access to financial services during the preparation process to claim the EITC.[32]

During the 2011 tax filing season, the Bureau provided materials to 3,500 VITA sites across the country, which collectively assisted over 3 million taxpayers. The Bureau sought to encourage these taxpayers to pre-commit to saving a portion of their refund at the time their taxes were

---

[30] Many of these collaborations involve the Bureau's fellow member agencies in the Financial Literacy and Education Commission.

[31] The VITA program offers free tax return preparation help to people who make $51,000 or less through IRS-certified volunteers, at sites located at community and neighborhood centers, libraries, schools, shopping malls, and other local venues. *See generally* Internal Revenue Serv., *Free Tax Return Preparation for You by Volunteers*, www.irs.gov/Individuals/Free-Tax-Return-Preparation-for-You-by-Volunteers (last visited June 27, 2013).

[32] *See* 12 U.S.C. § 5493(d)(2)(F).

being prepared by providing training information for VITA tax preparers about how to talk about savings, and through three strategies:

- **Priming:** The Bureau developed a poster intended to suggest the idea of saving to taxpayers before they were asked to make a savings decision.

- **Pre-commitment:** While their taxes were being prepared, taxpayers were given a worksheet to help them determine how much they could comfortably save.

- **Automation:** Taxpayers were encouraged to direct-deposit a portion of their refunds into a savings account or savings bonds.

The Bureau built on these efforts in the 2012 tax filing season. For example, we updated the 2011 training materials, poster, and worksheet and made them available to VITA tax preparers via online fulfillment or download, which enables us to measure how many tax preparers obtain the materials.

3.2.2 K-12 financial education

In April 2013, the Bureau launched an initiative to build the financial capability of youth, and thus future generations of American consumers. This initiative seeks to foster inclusion of financial education in K-12 curriculum and facilitate teacher training in financial education. To launch the initiative, the Office of Financial Education hosted a national conference of financial education experts, teachers, and non-profit and governmental leaders

> Schools provide the opportunity to transform the financial lives of a generation of Americans by introducing key money and finance-related concepts early, and building on that foundation through the K-12 years.

from local, state, and federal levels involved in K-12 financial education.[33] Recognizing the broad range of work that others already are doing in this field, the initiative seeks to strengthen the impact and effectiveness of K-12 financial education efforts by fostering the sharing of, and building upon, best practices; facilitating partnerships; and collectively identifying, and seeking

---

[33] Conference proceedings are expected to be available on the Bureau's website in August 2013.

to fill, critical gaps. Conference panels addressed defining a shared vision, promising practices in integrating financial education in schools, the use of hands-on approaches, and research and evaluation to document the effectiveness of classroom financial education. The Bureau issued a white paper recommending strategies to improve personal financial management capability of youth, which is available at http://files.consumerfinance.gov/f/201304_cfpb_OFE-Policy-White-Paper-Final.pdf.[34]

3.2.3 Foundations: building an effective financial workplace

Through a joint effort between the Bureau's Office of Financial Education and Office of Human Capital, the Bureau is developing a financial education program to help employees become effective managers of their personal finances. Using findings from recent workplace research studies, the effort will combine tools such as automatic enrollment in retirement plans with financial planning assistance and other educational resources. The goal is to develop effective practices in the workplace that can be shared with other federal agencies as well as state and local governments and private sector employers.[35]

3.2.4 Work with faith-based communities

Understanding the role that faith-based communities play in building neighborhoods and supporting their members, the Office of Financial Education, in coordination with the Office of Community Affairs within the Division of External Affairs, is holding a series of webinars in 2013 with leaders of faith-based organizations to introduce participants to CFPB's financial education tools and resources.

---

[34] *See* CFPB, *Transforming the Financial Lives of a Generation of Young Americans: Policy Recommendations for Advancing K-12 Financial Education* (April 2013), *available at* http://files.consumerfinance.gov/f/201304_cfpb_OFE-Policy-White-Paper-Final.pdf. The approach of introducing key financial concepts early and continuing to build on that foundation throughout the K-12 years aligns with the Financial Literacy and Education Commission's 2013-2014 strategic focus on "Starting Early for Financial Success." *See supra* page 24.

[35] This program also aligns with the Financial Literacy and Education Commission's "Starting Early for Financial Success" strategic focus, which includes an Early Career and Retirement component aimed at helping Americans plan and act for long-term financial well-being early in their careers by promoting financial education and capability in the workplace.

3.2.5 Financial emergency preparedness: partnership with the Federal Emergency Management Agency

The Office of Financial Education has partnered with the Federal Emergency Management Agency (FEMA) to help consumers make informed financial decisions when preparing for and recovering from natural or manmade disasters. FEMA consulted with the Bureau as it prepared a financial preparedness page on its website, which is available at ready.gov/financialpreparedness. The Bureau also joined FEMA in a webinar about financial preparedness decision making, which was presented to 939 participants representing community groups, emergency assistance workers, faith-based organizations, and others. The Bureau also provided input and a resources link for an Emergency Financial First Aid Kit to be issued by FEMA.

3.2.6 Servicemembers

DEFENSE TRANSITION ASSISTANCE PROGRAM

In February 2012, Assistant Director Holly Petraeus received a request from Pentagon officials asking the Office of Servicemember Affairs to assist in the creation of financial planning materials for all servicemembers leaving the military. Experts from throughout the CFPB worked with Servicemember Affairs to provide content for the Department of Defense Transition Assistance Program curriculum. All of the military services are using this material to assist servicemembers with the financial aspects of planning for a career change. The feedback during the user testing period ranked the financial education module as the most popular activity during the week-long transition training workshop.

JUDGE ADVOCATE GENERAL'S CORPS TRAINING

Servicemember Affairs' education efforts have included providing subject-matter expertise to the military legal community. Bureau staff provided instruction on several occasions at The Judge Advocate General's Legal Center and School located in Charlottesville, Virginia. The Offices of Servicemember Affairs and Students also teamed up to provide instruction about consumer risk in the student loan marketplace during an October 2012 legal assistance training course. These efforts help advance the Office of Servicemember Affairs' educational reach by leveraging the extensive consumer law mission of the Judge Advocate General's Corps.

DELAYED ENTRY PROGRAM

In September 2012, the Office of Servicemember Affairs began developing a "just enough and just in time" financial education experience to equip Delayed Entry Program (DEP) participants with the information and education needed to make sound financial decisions in certain target subject areas. DEP participants are individuals who have committed to join the military but have not yet reported to boot camp. Our DEP education program aims to offer experiential education that engages the interest and caters to the learning style of the recruit demographic. The Bureau and the Department of Defense will work together to make course content and materials available across the varied timelines and geographical locations of future recruits and across the armed services. Introducing the Bureau as a resource to recruits through DEP should also set the stage for future financial education efforts.

VIRTUAL FINANCIAL EDUCATION FORUM ON STUDENT LOANS

In March 2013, the Office of Servicemember Affairs teamed up with the Office for Students and the Office of Consumer Engagement to deliver the Bureau's first military-focused virtual financial education forum by means of live webcast. The forum reached nearly 300 military financial educators, legal assistance attorneys, and on-base college education counselors. Participants learned about student loan servicing issues for servicemembers and CFPB resources available to assist them. Content highlights from the event were relayed through social media channels with a potential reach of approximately 25,000 individuals. External social media partnerships with the Department of Defense and the Military Family Learning Network were used to amplify the message to servicemembers stationed overseas, including individuals at military bases located from the Middle East (Turkey) to East Asia (Okinawa) and a deployed U.S. Navy unit operating off the coast of West Africa.

MILITARY SAVES WEEK

The Office of Servicemember Affairs used Military Saves Week in February 2012 as an opportunity to distribute a video message to military units about the importance of saving for goals. Military units are able to download the video from YouTube and post it on their own social media channels. To date, there have been over 2,000 views of the video directly on YouTube.

3.2.7 Students

FINANCIAL AID SHOPPING SHEET

The Bureau partnered with the Department of Education to develop a "Financial Aid Shopping Sheet" to help students and their parents make informed decisions about how to finance postsecondary educational expenses.[36] Financial aid offers from colleges and universities often fail to make basic information clear, such as how much of a particular aid offer is made up of loans that need to be paid back and how much comes from grants that do not. The Higher Education Opportunity Act of 2008 required the Secretary of Education to develop a model financial aid offer format to help students and their parents make informed decisions about how to finance postsecondary educational expenses.[37] The shared mission to improve the shopping process for potential student borrowers made the CFPB and the Department of Education natural partners in a Know Before You Owe project on student loans.

The Financial Aid Shopping Sheet is a standardized, easy-to-read form of financial aid award letter that colleges and universities can send to prospective students. The Shopping Sheet is designed to allow college applicants to better understand the debt implications of their college choice and compare the costs of the schools to which they apply.

The agencies released a prototype shopping sheet in October 2011. The Secretary of Education released the finalized Financial Aid Shopping Sheet in July 2012, and published an open letter to college and university presidents, calling for schools to voluntarily adopt the shopping sheet.

In April 2012, the President of the United States issued an Executive Order requiring colleges that accept Department of Defense Tuition Assistance Program funds to provide military students with an offer letter based on the principles developed for the Financial Aid Shopping Sheet, in order to provide better information to recipients of military and veteran education benefits.[38] The Executive Order also encourages colleges that accept Post-9/11 G.I. Bill benefits

---

[36] The Financial Aid Shopping Sheet is available at http://collegecost.ed.gov/shopping_sheet.pdf.

[37] Higher Education Opportunity Act of 2008, Pub. L. No. 110-315, § 484, 122 Stat. 3078, 3286 (codified at 20 U.S.C. § 1092 note).

[38] Exec. Order No. 13607, 77 Fed. Reg. 25,861 (Apr. 27, 2012).

to do the same. As of May 2013, 737 colleges and universities, with a combined enrollment of 3.47 million students, had voluntarily agreed to adopt the Financial Aid Shopping Sheet.

3.2.8 Older Americans

ELDER JUSTICE COORDINATING COUNCIL

The Bureau serves as a member agency of the Elder Justice Coordinating Council. The Elder Justice Coordinating Council was established by the Elder Justice Act of 2009 to coordinate activities related to elder abuse, neglect, and exploitation across relevant Federal, state, local, and private agencies and entities.[39] The Council is chaired by the Secretary of Health and Human Services (HHS), and the CFPB is one of 11 member agencies, in addition to HHS, that HHS has identified for membership based on their administering programs related to abuse, neglect, or financial exploitation of older Americans. The Bureau, through its Office for Older Americans, is coordinating and building cooperative plans with its Council partners to address mistreatment of elders. Older Americans' staff members serve on the Elder Justice Interagency Working Group that staffs the Council. The Working Group is developing recommendations and proposed action steps for the Council based on white papers that were submitted by expert witnesses at the Council's inaugural meeting in October 2012.

FINANCIAL CRIMES ENFORCEMENT NETWORK

As an outgrowth of meetings between the Office for Older Americans and the Financial Crimes Enforcement Network (FinCEN), a component of the U.S. Department of the Treasury, FinCEN developed a report detailing incidences and trends in elder financial exploitation reflected in Suspicious Activity Reports (SARs) that financial institutions sent to FinCEN between February 2011 and August 2012.[40] The May 2013 issue of the SAR Activity Review, a bi-annual FinCEN publication, includes a summary analysis of the elder financial exploitation report and a

---

[39] Pub. L. No. 111-148, § 6703, 124 Stat. 119, 782 (codified at 42 U.S.C. § 1397k).

[40] FinCEN receives and encourages the use of SARs for reporting cases of suspected elder financial exploitation. *See* Financial Crimes Enforcement Network, Advisory to Financial Institutions on Filing Suspicious Activity Reports, FIN-2011-A003 (Feb. 22, 2011), *available at* http://www.fincen.gov/statutes_regs/guidance/pdf/fin-2011-a003.pdf.

"Message from the Office for Older Americans."[41] Helping to heighten awareness of elder financial exploitation among financial institutions that have Bank Secrecy Act reporting obligations can help to protect the public, since financial institution staff often speak directly with older consumers who are making large withdrawals or transfers of funds in response to financial scams.

OLDER AMERICAN PROTECTION NETWORKS

The Office for Older Americans is assisting older American protection networks of state and local governments, elder justice advocates, law enforcement agencies, financial service providers, and other key stakeholders that are working to improve community response to elder financial exploitation. The primary goals of the networks are to increase prevention of, and improve collaboration and response to, elder financial exploitation. The Office for Older Americans staff has been monitoring and participating in network activities such as community education events; and public awareness campaigns and cross-training programs for stakeholders, first responders, advocates, and industry professionals.

MONEY SMART FOR OLDER ADULTS

The CFPB and the Federal Deposit Insurance Corporation (FDIC) have developed Money Smart for Older Adults (MSOA), a curriculum for the FDIC's Money Smart program to provide older consumers and their caregivers with information on preventing and responding to elder financial exploitation.[42] Older Americans and the FDIC will offer several train-the-trainer webinars on the FDIC's Money Smart online training platform. Older Americans will also provide primers and train-the-trainer sessions to national non-profit organizations that have expressed interest in becoming Money Smart Alliance partners for the

> **Money Smart for Older Adults provides information for older adults and their caregivers on preventing and responding to elder financial exploitation.**

---

[41] Financial Crimes Enforcement Network, The SAR Activity Review, Trends Tips and Issues (May 2013), *available at* http://www.fincen.gov/news_room/rp/files/sar_tti_23.pdf.

[42] Money Smart is a financial education curriculum designed to help low- and moderate-income individuals enhance their financial skills. *See* FDIC, *Money Smart – A Financial Education Program*, http://www.fdic.gov/consumers/consumer/moneysmart/index.html (last visited June 27, 2013).

distribution of MSOA. The program was released in June 2013. Participant guides are available for download at files.consumerfinance.gov/f/201306_cfpb_msoa-participant-guide.pdf, or for order at promotions.usa.gov/cfpbpubs.html. Instructor materials are available from the FDIC at fdic.gov/consumers/consumer/moneysmart/olderadult.html.

3.2.9 Traditionally underserved consumers

The Office of Financial Empowerment is working to integrate financial empowerment strategies into existing public-sector and non-profit programs that assist low-income and economically vulnerable people who comprise the traditionally underserved.

FINANCIAL EMPOWERMENT TOOLKIT AND TRAINING

The Office of Financial Empowerment is developing a toolkit for front-line staff in organizations that provide direct social services to consumers. The toolkit will provide staff with tools to incorporate financial-empowerment support into their work with their clients and to make effective referrals to specialized providers. The toolkit includes information that staff can share with clients on topics such as emergency savings; understanding, correcting, and building credit history; managing debt; cash flow budgeting; and identifying financial products to use to pursue various financial and life goals. The toolkit also includes worksheets and other tools individuals can use to strengthen their personal money management skills. A pilot program is projected for fall of 2013. Workshops in local communities and internal staff trainings within national organizations are projected to reach over 6,000 caseworkers and other front-line staff by mid-fiscal year 2015. These staff members, in turn, have the potential capacity to reach up to 80,000 low-income and economically vulnerable clients.

FOSTER YOUTH CREDIT REPORTS

The Child and Family Services Improvement and Innovation Act requires that each child age 16 and older in foster care receive annually a free copy of any consumer credit report pertaining to the child until the child is discharged from foster care, and receive assistance in interpreting and resolving any inaccuracies in the report.[43] State and county child welfare agencies are currently

---

[43] Child and Family Services Improvement and Innovation Act, Pub. L. No. 112-34, § 106, 125 Stat. 369 (Sept. 30, 2011) (codified at 42 U.S.C. § 675(5)(I)); see 42 U.S.C. § 671(a)(16).

working with the national credit reporting agencies to implement these requirements. The Office of Financial Empowerment is working with stakeholders at the Federal Trade Commission and the Department of Health and Human Services Children's Bureau to help streamline the credit report-pulling procedures for child welfare agencies, and assist them in developing capacity to appropriately assist foster youth in identifying identity theft, fraud, and errors, and understanding and resolving inaccuracies in the reports.

4. Research and innovation: identifying what works

The Bureau is developing and implementing initiatives to educate and empower consumers to make better-informed financial decisions. This requires that we know what approaches are effective in improving financial decision making and financial well-being. There has been a growing realization among experts in financial education, however, that there is not enough evidence-based evaluation to indicate which financial education strategies are most effective. According to a 2011 Government Accountability Office (GAO) report on financial literacy, "[r]elatively few evidence-based evaluations of financial literacy programs have been conducted, limiting what is known about which specific methods and strategies are most effective."[44] The CFPB is taking up this challenge to provide stronger evidence of what works, in order to support and guide efforts to improve the effectiveness and quality of financial education, and therefore improve consumer decision making and outcomes.

> **The Bureau is conducting research to build on current knowledge of what approaches to financial education are effective and how to measure effectiveness.**

The Bureau is pursuing a research agenda to help inform its financial education work and ultimately to serve consumers. From a statutory perspective, there are a number of mandates that are served by the Bureau's financial education research strategy. For example, the Dodd-Frank Act requires the Office of Financial Education, together with the Office of Research, to

---

[44] U.S. Government Accountability Office, GAO-11-614, *Financial Literacy: A Federal Certification Process for Providers Would Pose Challenges* (June 28, 2011), at Highlights, *available at* http://www.gao.gov/assets/330/320203.pdf.

"conduct research related to consumer financial education and counseling."[45] The statute also charges the Office for Older Americans with conducting research to identify "best practices and effective methods, tools, technologies and strategies to educate and counsel seniors about personal finance management . . . ."[46] In addition, the Bureau's strategy to include research as a tool to improve the financial literacy of consumers is consistent with FLEC's National Strategy.[47]

The Office of Financial Education, in coordination with the Office of Research, has developed a research program that focuses on (1) determining how to measure financial well-being, and identifying the knowledge, skills, and habits associated with financially capable consumers, (2) evaluating the effectiveness of existing approaches to improving financial decision making and outcomes, and (3) developing and evaluating new approaches. Current projects are focused on the following:

- Evaluating the effectiveness of financial coaching programs and identifying the specific elements that are effective and why;

- Developing measures of financial well-being for working age and older Americans, and determining what types of knowledge, skills, and habits are associated with those measures of financial well-being;

- Piloting and evaluating approaches to enhance the financial capability of low-income and economically vulnerable consumers by integrating financial capability-enhancing products or services with other types of financial products and services that consumers want or use; and

---

[45] 12 U.S.C. § 5493(d)(3)(B).

[46] 12 U.S.C. § 5493(g)(3)(D).

[47] *See* Financial Literacy & Education Commission, *Promoting Financial Success in the United States: National Strategy for Financial Literacy 2011*, at 11 (Goal 4), *available at* http://www.treasury.gov/resource-center/financial-education/Documents/NationalStrategyBook_12310%20(2).pdf.

- Piloting and evaluating innovative approaches to address common consumer financial decision-making challenges.

These projects are described further below.

4.1 Financial education evaluation project

The Bureau is conducting a quantitative evaluation of two existing financial coaching programs. Financial coaching generally involves one-on-one sessions with clients to increase clients' awareness of their financial decisions and to provide support for clients to reach financial goals mutually set by the coach and client.[48]

Based upon preliminary evidence of the programs' effectiveness, their willingness to participate in a rigorous evaluation, program size, diversity of geography and client base, and other factors, the CFPB selected two community-based financial coaching providers for the evaluation. The evaluation will use a randomized control trial to determine the extent to which the selected sites' financial coaching strategies increase household non-retirement savings and reduce financial distress among program participants. The two evaluations have begun, and final results are expected in early 2015.

The project also includes a peer-learning component, comprising a network of eight financial education programs focused on improving financial decision making and outcomes, and researchers engaged in rigorous evaluation of the programs. The first meeting of the peer-learning network was held in April 2013. The meeting facilitated the sharing of programmatic best practices and evaluation methodologies that promote effective financial education evaluation.

---

[48] *See generally* University of Wisconsin Cooperative Extension, Financial Coaching Strategies, http://fyi.uwex.edu/financialcoaching/what-is-coaching/ (last visited June 27, 2013).

4.2 Measuring financial well-being

The CFPB is conducting a research project to develop measures of financial well-being for working age and older American consumers. To this end, the project is focused on learning:

- What knowledge and behavior predict financial well-being;

- The importance of financial knowledge relative to other factors (personal traits and social context) in improving financial well-being; and,

- How to effectively measure financial knowledge, behavior, and well-being in order to assess consumer financial well-being and effectiveness of financial education.

The Bureau has completed background research and developed a detailed qualitative research plan, to be implemented in 2013, to develop definitions of financial well-being for working-age and older Americans and hypotheses regarding the drivers of financial well-being. The qualitative research will involve interviews and surveys with both consumers and various types of financial professionals, such as financial educators, advisers, planners, coaches, tax preparers, and credit counselors. In 2014, the Bureau will create survey items to test the hypotheses it has developed about the determinants of financial well-being. The next step will be to use the survey items to qualitatively test the hypotheses.

The products of this project should allow the CFPB, other government agencies, and others involved in financial education to further hone informed approaches to improving consumer financial well-being. Further, by creating or vetting rigorously developed measures of consumer financial knowledge, behavior, well-being, and related factors, the project will create a strong basis for evaluating financial education policies and programs. More specifically, these metrics should significantly increase the ability of the CFPB, other government agencies, and other financial education providers to select approaches that make the biggest difference in improving consumer outcomes.

4.3 Building financial capability through product design and program delivery

The Office of Financial Empowerment is conducting a three-phase research, evaluation, and pilot project that will help the Bureau determine whether the financial capability of low-income and economically vulnerable consumers can be enhanced through bundled financial products (such as a prepaid card that also has a savings function) and/or integration of financial coaching and counseling into the offering of financial products.

The Bureau is currently completing the research phase of the project. This research has entailed a scan of the field to build a comprehensive database of existing strategies, products, or programs that seek to help consumers build positive credit histories and savings through bundled products and bundled services; a literature review of existing research on savings and credit building strategies, products, or programs focused on economically vulnerable consumers; and a report documenting findings of discussions with academic and practitioner experts on types of barriers for consumers, program features that overcome those barriers, and recommendations for specific types of programs the Bureau should consider for evaluation. The second phase of the project, scheduled to begin in summer 2013, will be a randomized control trial of two programs, designed to determine whether the programs are successful in building the credit histories and/or savings of economically vulnerable consumers. The third phase, expected to begin in 2015, will be a pilot project involving two "ideal case" approaches identified in the research and evaluation stages.

4.4 Innovation pilots project

A wide range of financial education and empowerment practices are currently in use by organizations and institutions that are involved in financial education, asset building, and related services. Many of these provide significant benefit to consumers. However, as discussed above, many American consumers are still struggling to manage their financial lives and make the financial decisions that will best serve their own life goals. Innovative approaches to financial education and financial empowerment can help consumers face these challenges.

Information alone is not always sufficient in leading to financial decisions that will serve one's life goals. According to a 2011 GAO report on financial literacy, "[i]nsights from behavioral economics, which blends economics with psychology, have been used to design strategies apart from education to assist consumers in reaching goals without compromising their ability to choose approaches or products."[49] This GAO report discusses effective practices such as changing the default option, using commitment mechanisms, simplifying decisions, and leveraging the impact of peer support and influence in leading to desirable consumer financial outcomes. Using such strategies has the potential to lead to more effective financial education and empowerment efforts.

In order to meet its goal of promoting effective financial education practices, the CFPB is conducting an innovation pilot project to develop prototypes of approaches to help consumers overcome common decision-making challenges and then evaluate the effectiveness of the approaches. When final results become available in 2014, the Bureau expects that this project will increase knowledge of innovative approaches to improve financial capability, which can strengthen financial education content and strategy both within the CFPB and among a range of external stakeholders who serve consumers. The project may also inform policy at the CFPB, by providing insights into how consumers respond to product features and other aspects of the decision-making context.

---

[49] *See* Government Accountability Office, GAO-11-614, *Financial Literacy: A Federal Certification Process for Providers Would Pose Challenges* (June 28, 2011), at 18, *available at* http://www.gao.gov/assets/330/320203.pdf.

5. Outreach: sharing information and forging relationships to reach consumers

In order to accomplish its financial education strategy, the Bureau is engaging extensively with consumers, as well as a wide range of organizations that interact with consumers in their financial lives or have insight into the financial challenges consumers face. These organizations, which include financial education providers, federal, state, and local government agencies, financial institutions, and various other private and non-profit organizations, are essential conduits through which we can reach and assist consumers. This outreach work both informs our strategy on an ongoing basis and enables us to forge relationships with organizations that are relevant to financial capability and that can deliver value to the public. More specifically, through our outreach efforts we do the following.

> The Bureau is engaging with a wide range of organizations in order to reach a larger portion of the American public with effective financial education resources.

- We introduce the Bureau, the financial education component of its mission, and its financial education resources to consumers, financial education providers, and others. This helps to make the Bureau known as a source for information and tools for navigating the financial marketplace, and as a potential partner for financial education initiatives and research.

- We learn about consumers' financial needs, aspirations, and experiences and the challenges that both consumers and financial education providers face, and hear recommendations for what the Bureau can do to improve consumers' financial capability or augment the efforts of existing financial education providers. This information informs the Bureau's financial education strategy and initiatives.

- We forge relationships and lay the groundwork for collaborative action, as we identify opportunities to leverage existing resources and strengthen existing approaches, or initiate new ones.

- We pave a two-way street for sharing information and developing comprehensive approaches, so that we can broadly share the fruits of our education and research and innovation initiatives, and the effective financial education and research work of other organizations, and amplify the effects of successful efforts.

Highlights of the Bureau's financial education outreach efforts are set forth below.

5.1 Financial education

During its first two years of operation, the Office of Financial Education engaged with consumers and a wide range of financial education providers and other stakeholders to introduce the Bureau and its financial education mission and resources, engage in a dialogue to shape its financial education strategy and initiatives, and build relationships for collaborative efforts. In addition to reaching 7.3 million consumers with tax refund inserts, the Office of Financial Education has reached more than 15,000 individuals through these efforts. Highlights include the following.

TAX REFUND INSERTS

In partnership with the Department of Treasury's Fiscal Bureau, the Office of Financial Education provided CFPB inserts for approximately 7.3 million tax refund checks. The inserts introduced the Bureau and its mission and provided information about how to access Ask CFPB for answers to questions about financial products and services and how to submit a complaint.

REQUEST FOR INFORMATION

The Office of Financial Education published a request for information on effective financial education in the Federal Register in August 2012, and received over 100 comments from organizations, individuals, financial institutions, and other entities addressing consumers' common financial decision-making challenges, common challenges in providing financial education, challenges around research and data, and promising practices and approaches.[50] In May 2013 the Bureau issued a report summarizing the comments and the results of the listening sessions. The report, Feedback from the Financial Education Field, is available at files.consumerfinance.gov/f/201305_cfpb_OFE-request-for-information-report.pdf.

LISTENING SESSIONS

The Office of Financial Education held a series of four listening sessions in 2012 with financial educators and financial institutions in New York, San Francisco, rural Mississippi, and St. Louis. The listening sessions in New York focused on general financial education topics, while the other sessions focused, respectively, on innovation in financial education, rural-specific concerns in financial education, and research needs in this field. Through these sessions, OFE met with approximately 120 individuals and organizations that collectively serve thousands of individual consumers.

MEETINGS WITH STAKEHOLDERS

The Office of Financial Education has conducted over 300 meetings with a wide range of key financial education stakeholders, including financial educators, community leaders, and organizations that could provide insight into financial education needs of consumers. These organizations included faith-based organizations; organizations that serve minority populations and/or communities of color, immigrant populations, rural communities, and Native Americans; and domestic and international financial education organizations. The meetings have focused on what challenges these stakeholders face when serving consumers and what the Bureau can do to help them better address the financial education needs of their constituencies.

WEBINARS

The Office of Financial Education has conducted a series of online presentations featuring experts within the CFPB in order to disseminate information about the CFPB and its financial education resources, and provide learning opportunities for financial education providers. These webinars have reached approximately 900 participants representing organizations such as

---

[50] *See* Request for Information on Effective Financial Education, 77 Fed. Reg. 46069 (Aug. 2, 2012), *available at* http://www.gpo.gov/fdsys/pkg/FR-2012-08-02/pdf/2012-18830.pdf.

financial institutions, academic institutions, non-profit organizations, and other government agencies that can use the resources to serve consumers directly, or share them with constituents that serve consumers. We further expand our reach by participating in webinars offered by other federal agencies and entities.

5.2 Servicemembers

Since its formation in January 2011, the CFPB's Office of Servicemember Affairs has conducted a wide range of outreach to deliver financial education information to military and veteran consumers and interested organizations, build a digital network, and build relationships with other federal agencies and state and local governments to serve the needs of servicemembers and veterans.

MILITARY INSTALLATION AND UNIT VISITS

Servicemember Affairs has conducted 112 outreach events, delivering consumer financial education information to more than 33,380 military and veteran consumers. These events have included reaching out to servicemembers where they live and work by visiting 51 military installations/National Guard units and participating in 20 town halls and 33 roundtable discussions with senior military leaders. At these events, Servicemember Affairs leadership and staff listened to servicemembers discuss the financial challenges they face, observed financial education training, and provided educational information.

EXTERNAL OUTREACH

The Office of Servicemember Affairs participated in 75 outreach events sponsored by external organizations seeking educational information about the office and the CFPB. Servicemember Affairs also delivered financial education information and updates about the work of the office through the Bureau's and other stakeholders' digital social media properties. Servicemember Affairs launched its own branded social media properties to serve the military and veteran communities in November 2012. Between launch and March 31, 2013, the channels reached an average of 4,356 users per week.

BUILDING A COLLABORATION NETWORK

The Office of Servicemember Affairs has worked with the Federal Trade Commission, Board of Governors of the Federal Reserve System, Federal Deposit Insurance Corporation, and Federal

Housing Finance Agency, and the Departments of Defense, Veterans Affairs, Justice, Housing and Urban Development, Education, Treasury, and Labor to raise awareness of the CFPB's mission and Servicemember Affairs' specific efforts on behalf of the military and veteran community. At the state level, the Bureau's efforts have centered on introducing state and local resources to the military community. Military consumer-focused events included the participation of twenty state National Guard Adjutants General and the Attorneys General of sixteen states. The Office of Servicemember Affairs has also established regular communications with all the state Directors of Veteran Affairs.

5.3 Students

The Office for Students engages with younger consumers and stakeholders throughout the higher education community by conducting direct outreach on college campuses, by hosting events with college students and student advocates, and by participating in conferences. The Office for Students has leveraged these relationships as distribution channels for the programs and products developed to help younger consumers make smarter choices in the marketplace.

STUDENT AND CAMPUS OUTREACH

The Office for Students meets regularly with students, campus leaders, and student advocates. To date the Office for Students has met in person with more than 600 individuals from organizations that collectively represent tens of thousands of students from over 20 states.

PAYING FOR COLLEGE DEMONSTRATIONS

In partnership with the Consumer Engagement team, the Office for Students has hosted webinars to demonstrate the features of our Paying for College suite of tools. These webinars are attended by a range of audiences including students, student advocates, financial aid advisers, and college counselors. Since the launch of the first Paying for College cost comparison tool in April 2012, the Office for Students has conducted more than a dozen webinars and in-person demonstrations.

CONFERENCE CALLS ABOUT STUDENT LOAN COMPLAINTS

In an effort to inform consumers about the complaint process and Consumer Response, the Office for Students sent letters to more than 7,000 college and university officials across the country, notified state banking regulators in all 50 states, and hosted a series of conference calls with student groups, college and university officials, consumer groups, and customer advocates at major financial institutions.

5.4 Older Americans

The Office for Older Americans has engaged in extensive outreach with older consumers and other stakeholders to learn what efforts have been underway to strengthen the financial literacy of older consumers, and to engage them in the office's work to help older consumers protect themselves from unfair, deceptive, and abusive practices and strengthen their financial capability with current and future financial choices. In furtherance of these goals, the Office for Older Americans has held or participated in over 200 events, which have been attended by more than 7,900 people. Participants have included, among others, older consumers, public officials, and representatives from financial institutions, the consumer services industry, consumer advocacy organizations, and other stakeholders. Highlights include the following.

PRESENTATIONS

The Office for Older Americans made presentations at the June 2012 World Elder Abuse Awareness Day conference at the White House; the State of Illinois' Elder Rights Conference; the Association of Anti-Money Laundering Specialists Conference; the annual meeting of the California District Attorneys Association; the Adult Abuse Training Institute/Hunter College (NY State); the Utah State Senior Expo; and the National Association of State Securities Administrators National Investor Education training conference for 120 state securities administrators. Older Americans also made presentations to the National Committee to Prevent Elder Abuse, the National Adult Protective Services Association, the National Center for Victims of Crime, and the National Federation of Community Development Credit Unions.

REQUEST FOR INFORMATION

The Office for Older Americans issued a request for information in the Federal Register in June 2012, and received over one thousand comments in response to specific questions about senior financial exploitation and financial literacy efforts, including questions about how to protect seniors from fraudulent or misleading use of senior designations by financial advisers to imply specialized expertise in financial planning for older consumers.[51]

LISTENING SESSIONS

The Office for Older Americans held public listening sessions in Washington, D.C. and San Francisco in 2012 to obtain input from consumer advocates, industry professionals, and regulators on the use of senior designations for financial advisers. These sessions helped inform the Bureau's findings and observations for its report and recommendations on the use of senior designations.[52]

RESEARCH ROUNDTABLE ON ELDER FINANCIAL EXPLOITATION

The Office for Older Americans convened an invitational, interdisciplinary Research Roundtable on Elder Financial Exploitation in April 2013. The goals of the Roundtable were to assess the current state of research on how to protect older Americans from financial exploitation; obtain input from experts on what additional research is needed to advance protections in this area; generate ideas on appropriate and promising research methodologies; and help the Bureau shape its own research agenda on this topic. Attendees included leading academic researchers on aging issues as well as colleagues from other federal agencies that are members of the Elder Justice Coordinating Council (Administration on Aging and National Institute on Aging, Department of Health and Human Services; Department of Justice; Social Security Administration).

5.5 Traditionally underserved consumers

A key aspect of the early and continuing work of the Office of Financial Empowerment has been outreach to entities at the local, state, and national level that are concerned with the financial stability of low-income and economically vulnerable people and their use of financial products

---

[51] 77 Fed. Reg. 36491 (June 19, 2012), *available at* http://www.gpo.gov/fdsys/pkg/FR-2012-06-19/pdf/2012-14854.pdfhttp://www.gpo.gov/fdsys/pkg/FR-2012-06-19/pdf/2012-14854.pdf.

[52] CFPB, *Senior Designations for Financial Advisers: Reducing Consumer Confusion and Risks* (April 18, 2013), *available at* http://files.consumerfinance.gov/f/201304_CFPB_OlderAmericans_Report.pdf.

and services, in order to inform Empowerment strategies. These organizations include social service agencies, municipal agencies, financial institutions, product developers, researchers, civil rights and consumer organizations, organizations that serve communities of color, and others.

NATIONAL FINANCIAL EMPOWERMENT CONVENING

In November 2012, the Office of Financial Empowerment brought together over 100 representatives of financial institutions, prudential regulators and other government agencies, consumer and civil rights organizations, municipal officials, local program administrators, researchers, and others for the Bureau's first national Financial Empowerment Convening. The working sessions of the convening were organized in three tracks representing the driving themes of Empowerment's work: access, data, and scale.

LISTENING SESSIONS

The Office of Financial Empowerment held listening sessions in San Francisco, Seattle, New York, St. Louis, Cincinnati, Dallas, and Louisville. At these sessions, 131 participants from 87 organizations shared information on their financial education/empowerment efforts and on low-income consumers' experience with financial products, including barriers in accessing credit and bank accounts and debt traps they encounter.

C.A.R.E. FREE HEALTH CLINIC, DALLAS, TEXAS

The Offices of Financial Empowerment and Financial Education participated in a one-day free health clinic attended by approximately 1,200 patients and 1,000 volunteers. Empowerment and Financial Education staff provided CFPB consumer financial education publications in English and Spanish to clinic patients and spoke to approximately 100 patients about financial issues.

OUTREACH CALLS/WEBINARS

On March 5, 2013, the Offices of Financial Empowerment and Financial Education hosted a webinar that reached over 300 Legal Aid and Legal Services entities. These "first responders" work with low-income and economically vulnerable consumers every day; their insights and information are important to understanding the financial challenges faced by these consumers. The webinar provided participants with information about the Bureau's consumer protection tools, including Ask CFPB and the complaint process.

6. Conclusion

All Americans, regardless of income and level of educational attainment, need to be able to evaluate the choices available to them in the financial marketplace and understand the implications of their financial decisions in order to build secure financial futures. The Bureau's statutory function to educate and empower consumers to make better informed financial decisions has created an enormous opportunity to reach consumers at the right moment with targeted information, tools, and signposts so that consumers can increase their financial management skills and money confidence. In its first two years, the Bureau has launched a broad range of initiatives to provide consumers with information, resources, and opportunities to develop the knowledge and skills to manage their financial resources effectively and plan for future life events. Working side by side with other governmental agencies, the private and non-profit sectors, schools, workplaces, and faith communities, the Bureau looks forward to continuing to serve the public in this manner in the years to come. Financially capable consumers are essential to fully and responsibly harness the financial system's tremendous capacity to enhance economic stability and opportunity to help all people in America to reach their life goals.

www.ingramcontent.com/pod-product-compliance
Lightning Source LLC
Chambersburg PA
CBHW081900170526
45167CB00007B/3090